WILLIAMS·SONOMA

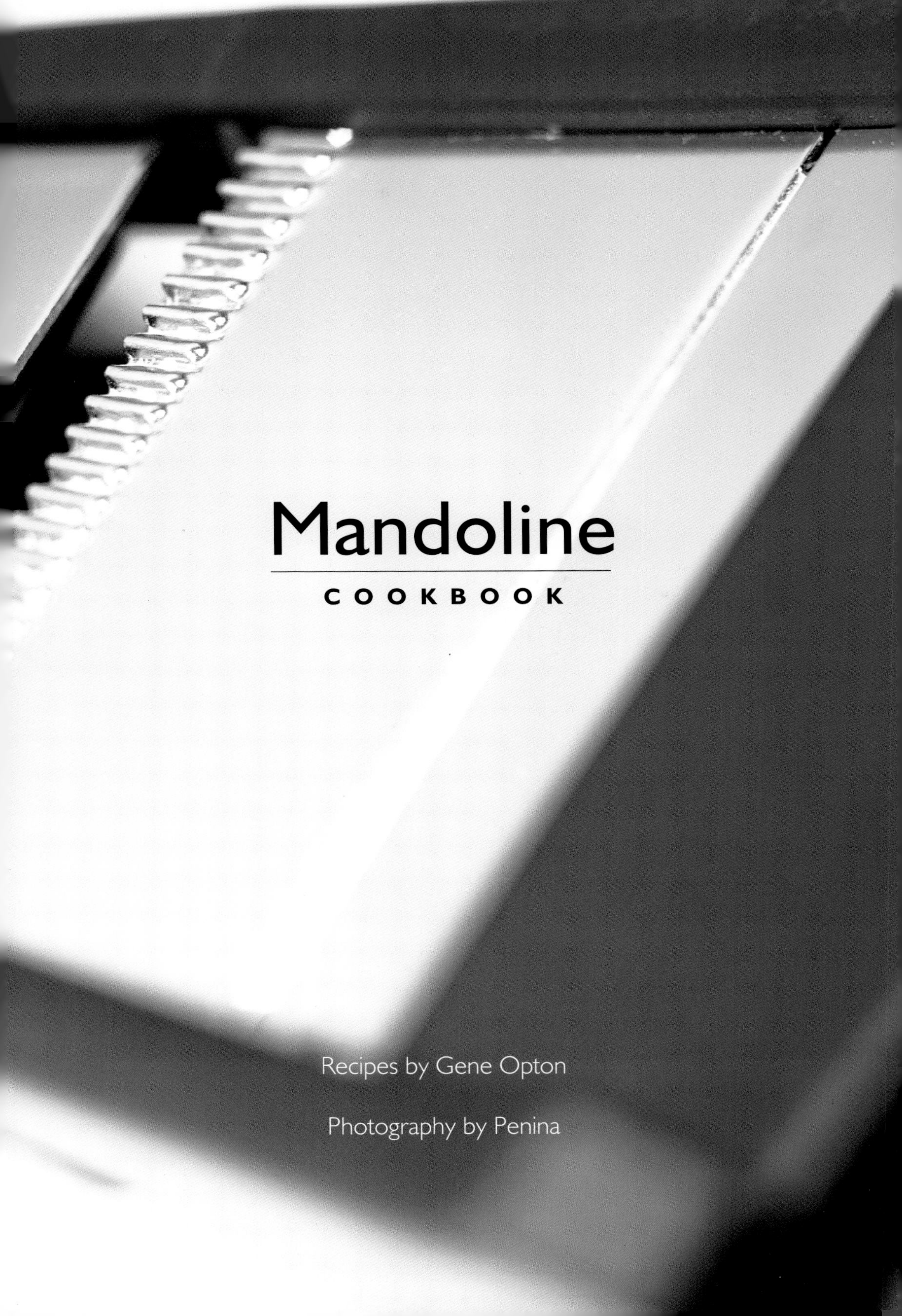

Mandoline

COOKBOOK

Recipes by Gene Opton

Photography by Penina

WILLIAMS-SONOMA
Founder and Vice Chairman: Chuck Williams
Book Buyer: Victoria Kalish

WELDON OWEN INC.
President: John Owen
Vice President and Publisher: Wendely Harvey
Chief Operating Officer: Larry Partington
Vice President International Sales: Stuart Laurence
Associate Publisher: Lisa Atwood
Managing Editor: Jan Newberry
Consulting Editor: Norman Kolpas
Copy Editors: Sharon Silva and Carolyn Miller
Design: Kari Perin, Perin+Perin
Production Director: Stephanie Sherman
Production Manager: Jen Dalton
Production Editor: Cecily Upton
Food Stylist: Sandra Cook
Prop Stylist: Sara Slavin

In collaboration with Williams-Sonoma
3250 Van Ness, San Francisco, CA 94109

A WELDON OWEN PRODUCTION

Library of Congress Cataloging-in-Publication Data

Opton, Gene.
    Mandoline cookbook / recipes by Gene Opton:
    photography by Penina.
        p. cm. -- (Williams-Sonoma cookware series)
    Includes index.
    ISBN 1-887451-13-7
        1. Mandoline (Utensils). I. Title. II. Series: Williams-
    Sonoma cookware.
TX840.M35068 1998
641.5'89 -- dc21   97-39427 CIP

First printed in 1998
10 9 8 7 6 5 4 3 2 1

Production by Toppan Printing Co. (H.K.), Ltd.
Printed in China

A Note on Weights and Measures:
All recipes include customary U.S. and metric
measurements. Metric conversions are based on
a standard developed for these books and have
been rounded off. Actual weights may vary.

CONTENTS

ABOUT THE MANDOLINE

Credit for developing the mandoline likely belongs to some impatient European chef who grew frustrated with his clumsy apprentices. The knife skills required to transform a mountain of potatoes into the uniform pieces needed to make pommes frites *or to trim a knob of celery root (celeriac) into perfect julienne strips for* céleri-rave rémoulade *take time and patience to acquire. But armed with a mandoline instead of a knife, a novice cook can cut vegetables as quickly and precisely as the most seasoned kitchen professional.*

Speed and precision are the main reasons for using a mandoline. With its straight slicing blade, serrated crinkle-waffle blade, narrow-toothed julienne blades, or wider-toothed french-fry blade locked securely in place, you can cut large quantities of identically sized slices or strips as quickly as you can move a vegetable or fruit back and forth along the mandoline's frame.

There are several different types of mandolines, but they all function according to the same basic principles. A long rectangular frame made of wood, brass, or, as shown here, sturdy composite fiberglass holds in place one of several stainless-steel cutting blades and a smooth guiding plate (stainless steel is the most common, although plastic and wood are also used). Using a knob or lever, the position of this plate is adjusted relative to the blade to make thinner or thicker slices.

Some basic mandolines are simply held at an angle on the work surface with one hand while the other hand moves the ingredient back and forth across the blade. Better mandolines include a fold-out stand that supports the frame securely at a comfortable angle on your kitchen counter and a hand guard that fits over the frame. A knob on top of the hand guard keeps your fingers clear of the cutting edge, and spikes on its underside firmly grip the ingredient while you move it across the mandoline blade.

It's important to note that the mandoline cuts some ingredients more easily than others. Firm textured foods such as potatoes, radishes, cucumbers, zucchini (courgettes), onions, beets, apples, and pears work well. More awkwardly shaped produce, such as cabbages, fennel, and mushrooms, move less smoothly along the mandoline's frame. Turnips and celery root, which tend to be woody when larger and older, sometimes require more forceful pushing across the blades—and therefore greater caution.

You should also be aware that using the mandoline often means trimming away good-sized edible portions of whatever food you are cutting. Use these leftovers to flavor stocks, add them to vegetable soups, turn them into garnishes for salads, or nibble on them while you work.

safety reminder

Mandoline blades are extremely sharp. As with any high-quality stainless-steel blades, they cut most efficiently and safely when well honed and may require professional resharpening from time to time. When installing or changing blades, always handle them with the utmost caution. Use the hand guard that comes with your mandoline or wrap your hand in a heavy kitchen towel and always keep your hands—particularly your fingertips—well away from the blades. Refer to the manufacturer's brochure for specific instructions on the care and safe use of your model.

MANDOLINE COMPONENTS

Most mandolines come with a re-movable, double-edged slicing blade, with one straight edge for slicing and an opposite serrated edge for making waffle and ruffle cuts. In addition, julienne and french-fry blades, in-serted in slots in the frame, work in conjunction with the main blade's straight edge to cut strips of varying widths. Use these various blades to make the kinds of cuts shown on pages 10–12.

STRAIGHT EDGE OF SLICING BLADE | The sharp, straight edge of the slicing blade will cut a variety of foods into neat, thin slices. Ad-just the knob or lever beneath the mandoline's guiding plate to cut slices so thin they are almost trans-parent or as thick as $1/4$ inch (6 mm). To make very thin slices, slide the slicing blade up the channel of the frame until the blade is approxi-mately $1/8$ inch (3 mm) from the bottom of the guiding plate. For thick slices, move the blade back down the frame.

SERRATED EDGE OF SLICING BLADE | On the side opposite the blade's straight edge is a sharp, serrated edge. To make crinkle-cut slices, adjust the height of the plate to a cutting thickness greater than the blade's $1/8$-inch (3-mm) thick-ness (page 10). To make waffle cuts,

adjust the guiding plate so that the slices are only slightly thicker than the serrated edge of the slicing blade and rotate the vegetable or fruit 90 degrees each time you slice. (See step-by-step instructions on page 11.) Note that when making waffle cuts, you cannot use the hand guard. To avoid injury, wrap your hand in a heavy kitchen towel before you begin slicing.

JULIENNE BLADES | These blades consist of sharp, triangular teeth positioned at right angles to the straight cutting edge of the slicing blade and are fitted into a slot on the side of the frame. As you move a fruit or vegetable down the guiding plate, the teeth and blade together cut it into thin strips. The thickness of the strips depends upon the thick-ness to which you set the guiding plate and on the number of teeth on the julienne blade you select. Stan-dard options are $1/8$ inch (3 mm) and $3/16$ inch (5 mm).

FRENCH-FRY BLADE | Designed to work in tandem with the straight edge of the slicing blade precisely like the julienne blades, the french-fry blade has its teeth set farther apart, at a distance of $3/8$ inch (10 mm). This is the perfect width for cutting potatoes into classically shaped french fries.

Straight Edge

Sliced Beets

Waffle-Cut Zucchini

Serrated Edge

1/8-inch (3-mm) Julienne Blade

Carrot Julienne

French-Fried Potatoes

French-Fry Blade

The type of cut you make is determined by which of the slicing blade's two sharpened edges faces the guiding plate: the straight edge produces smooth slices (below), and the serrated edge makes both crinkle cuts (bottom) and waffle cuts (opposite). Before you begin slicing, trim the vegetable or fruit and cut it in half or quarters if necessary to make pieces that can be gripped securely by the hand guard and will glide easily across the guiding plate.

One important note of caution when making waffle cuts: since you must rotate the vegetable 90 degrees after every stroke, you cannot use the hand guard when cutting them. Work with long sections of vegetable to keep your fingers far from the blade, and when the piece gets short, put it aside for another use and begin again with another long section. Work deliberately, pay close attention, and do not cut too quickly.

regular slices

Position the slicing blade with the straight edge facing the guiding plate. Set the guiding plate to the desired thickness. Secure the ingredient beneath the hand guard. Cut a test slice and adjust the thickness if necessary. Continue slicing.

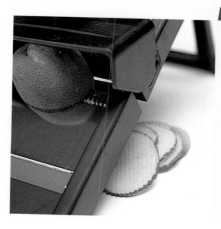

crinkle cut

Position the slicing blade with the serrated edge facing the guiding plate. Set the guiding plate to a thickness greater than 1/8 inch (3 mm). Secure the ingredient beneath the hand guard. Cut a test slice and adjust the thickness if necessary to yield neat crinkle-cut slices. Continue slicing.

waffle cut

Position the slicing blade with the serrated edge facing the guiding plate. Set the guiding plate to a thickness slightly greater than 1/8 inch (3 mm). Holding the vegetable cut side down, and with your fingers well clear of the mandoline, push the vegetable downward across the blade.

Check the first slice: it should be a very thin crinkle cut. Rotate the vegetable 90 degrees and slice again. The next slice should be a waffle cut, with a grid of ridges and holes. If necessary, adjust the guiding plate. Continue slicing, rotating the vegetable 90 degrees with each slice.

potato chips

SERVES 2–4

2 russet potatoes,
1/2–3/4 lb (250–375 g) each

vegetable oil

salt to taste

Have ready a bowl three-fourths full of cold water. Trim ends of the potatoes flat, then cut the potatoes in half cross-wise. Set the straight edge of the slicing blade of the mandoline for very thin slices, 1/16 inch (2 mm) thick or less. Secure the hand guard on the trimmed end of a potato half, and slice the potato. Transfer the slices to the water as soon as they are cut; repeat with the remaining halves. Let the slices soak for at least 5 minutes to remove excess starch.

Meanwhile, pour vegetable oil to a depth of 2 inches (5 cm) into a deep, heavy saucepan. Heat the oil to 330°F (170°C) on a deep-frying thermometer.

Drain the potatoes and pat dry with paper towels. A handful at a time, fry the potatoes until pale gold, about 3 minutes. Transfer to a paper towel–lined tray and leave for at least 10 minutes or up to 2 hours. Leave the oil in the pan.

Just before serving, reheat the oil to 370°F (188°C). A handful at a time, fry the potatoes until golden brown and crisp, 3–4 minutes. Using tongs, transfer to a paper towel–lined tray and sprinkle with salt.

To make waffle-cut potato chips, cut the potatoes into waffles following the directions at left and fry as directed.

JULIENNE AND FRENCH-FRY BLADES

Any cook who has ever spent hours at a cutting board learning to trim vegetables into neat, even strips with a knife will appreciate working with the mandoline's julienne and french-fry blades. Lock one of the three multitoothed blades in place, and it is possible to slice multiple uniform strips in widths of ⅛ inch (3 mm), ³/₁₆ inch (5 mm), or ³/₈ inch (10 mm) with a single motion.

These blades work with the straight edge of the slicing blade. The straight edge cuts a slice, while the teeth of the julienne or french-fry blades divide it into even strips.

Before you cut an ingredient into julienne strips, first trim it into sections as long as the desired length of the strips (3–6 inches/7.5–15 cm), and then simply slice it lengthwise on the mandoline.

julienne

Position the slicing blade straight edge up. Insert a julienne blade into the mandoline. Position the ingredient beneath the hand guard. Make a sample slice, check the size of the strips, and adjust the guiding plate if necessary. Continue cutting.

french-fry

Position the slicing blade straight edge up; set the guiding plate to ³/₈ inch (10 mm). Insert the french-fry blade into the slot in the side of the frame. Cut a potato in half lengthwise and position it parallel to the frame. Using the hand guard, push down to cut fries.

french fries

SERVES 4

2 lb (1 kg) russet potatoes

vegetable oil

salt to taste

Have ready a bowl three-fourths full of cold water. Cut the potatoes in half lengthwise. Insert the ³⁄₈-inch (10-mm) french-fry blade next to the straight edge of the slicing blade and set the guiding plate to a thickness of ³⁄₈ inch (10 mm). Secure the hand guard on the uncut side of a potato half and slice the potato. Immediately transfer the cut pieces to the bowl of water and repeat with the remaining potatoes. Let the potatoes soak for at least 5 minutes.

Meanwhile, pour oil to a depth of 2 inches (5 cm) into a deep, heavy saucepan. Heat to 330°F (170°C) on a deep-frying thermometer.

Drain the potatoes and pat dry with paper towels. A handful at a time, fry the potatoes until pale gold, 4–5 minutes. Using a wire-mesh skimmer, transfer to a paper towel–lined tray and leave for at least 10 minutes or up to 2 hours. Leave the oil in the pan.

Just before serving, reheat the oil to 370°F (188°C). A handful at a time, fry the potatoes again until golden brown, 3–5 minutes. Using a wire-mesh skimmer, transfer to a paper towel–lined tray and sprinkle with salt. Serve hot.

soak potatoes

Excess starch in potatoes can inhibit browning. By soaking cut potatoes briefly in cold water, you can rinse away some of the starch. Be sure that the potatoes are dry before you fry. Wet potatoes will absorb more grease and can cause the oil to splatter.

cook them twice

Fry the potatoes at 330°F (170°C) to draw out excess moisture and partially cook them. Let the potatoes cool and then fry a second time at 370°F (188°C) to make crisp, golden french fries.

STARTERS

Shrimp Sauté with Waffle-Cut Zucchini, Corn, and Peppers

SERVES 6

This beautiful sauté, which includes waffle cuts,
julienne strips, and corn sliced right off the cob, shows
off the versatility of the mandoline.

2 zucchini (courgettes), trimmed

2 ears of corn

1 red bell pepper (capsicum)

3 tablespoons unsalted butter

2 cloves garlic, crushed

³/₄ lb (375 g) shrimp (prawns), peeled with tail segments
intact and deveined (about 24)

2 tablespoons corn oil

2 jalapeño chiles, halved, seeded, and thinly sliced

¹/₂ teaspoon salt

3 tablespoons minced fresh cilantro (fresh coriander)

Set the serrated edge of the slicing blade for a thickness slightly greater than ¹/₈ inch (3 mm). Make one slice of the zucchini, rotate the zucchini 90 degrees, and slice again to make a waffle cut. Repeat with the remaining zucchini.

Set the straight edge of the slicing blade to the depth of the kernels of corn. Holding the ear at the top, slice the kernels off the cob, rotating it as you work. Repeat with the remaining ear.

Insert the ¹/₈-inch (3-mm) julienne blade and adjust the guiding plate to ¹/₈ inch (3 mm). Holding the bell pepper with one side against the guiding plate, slice it, rotating it as you work.

In a frying pan over medium-high heat, warm the butter and garlic. When the butter foams, add the shrimp and cook, stirring occasionally, until just opaque, about 5 minutes. Transfer the shrimp to a plate and keep warm. Wipe the frying pan clean.

(continued on next page)

Shrimp Sauté with Waffle-Cut
Zucchini, Corn, and Peppers

(continued from previous page)

In the same pan over medium-high heat, warm the oil. When hot, add the zucchini and sauté, stirring occasionally, just until it begins to change color, about 2 minutes. Push the zucchini to one side of the pan, add the corn, and cook, stirring, until the kernels begin to darken, about 3 minutes. Add the bell pepper strips and the jalapeño slices and cook, stirring, until they soften slightly, about 1 minute longer. Season with the salt, tossing the vegetables lightly.

Transfer to warmed individual plates. Top with the shrimp and sprinkle the cilantro on top. Serve warm. ✳

Oven-Baked Potato Chips with Goat Cheese and Sun-Dried Tomatoes

MAKES ABOUT 3 DOZEN; SERVES 12

Slices of unpeeled potato, brushed with olive oil and baked crisp, make a base for savory morsels to pass at a party.
Try other toppings, too: sour cream and salsa, crème fraîche and caviar, smoked salmon and capers, or tapenade.

1 russet potato, unpeeled, ends trimmed,
and halved crosswise

2 tablespoons olive oil

salt and ground pepper to taste

2 large, oil-packed sun-dried tomatoes, drained

3 oz (90 g) plain or flavored fresh goat cheese

Preheat an oven to 375°F (190°C). Lightly brush an 11-by-16-inch (28-by-40-cm) rimmed baking sheet with olive oil.

Set the straight edge of the slicing blade for $^1/_8$ inch (3 mm) and slice the potato. Place the potato slices on the prepared baking sheet in a single layer and brush the tops with the olive oil. Sprinkle with salt and pepper.

Bake until golden brown, 15–20 minutes. If some of the potatoes cook faster than others, transfer those slices to a rack and return the rest to the oven. When all the slices are ready, transfer them to the rack immediately upon removing them from the oven. Let cool. (These chips can be made a day ahead and stored, tightly covered, at room temperature until needed.)

Cut the sun-dried tomatoes into strips $^1/_4$ inch (6 mm) wide. Spread a scant teaspoon of goat cheese in the center of each potato chip, making a depression in the center of the cheese. Fill with a piece or two of tomato and serve. ✳

Celery Root and Yellow Beet Terrine

*Boldly colored yellow beets (which do not bleed like red ones)
and their delicious green leaves enliven this celery root
and cheese mousse. The colorful terrine tastes equally good
served hot or at room temperature.*

2 yellow beets with greens intact,
about ½ lb (250 g) total weight

1 large celery root (celeriac), about 1½ lb (750 g),
peeled and cut into chunks

2 tablespoons unsalted butter

3 eggs

½ cup (2 oz/60 g) shredded mild cheddar cheese

½ cup (2 oz/60 g) shredded provolone cheese

¼ cup (1 oz/30 g) grated Parmesan cheese

1 teaspoon grated yellow onion

salt and ground pepper to taste

20

Trim off the beet greens, leaving about ⅛ inch (3 mm) stem on
each beet intact. Remove the beet leaves from their stalks and
rinse thoroughly; discard any battered ones. Place the leaves in
a frying pan with only the rinsing water clinging to them. Cover
and steam over medium heat until wilted, 2–3 minutes. Transfer the leaves to paper towels, spreading them out to dry and
patting off any excess moisture.

Place the beets in a saucepan, add water to cover, and bring to a
boil over high heat. Reduce the heat to medium and cook until
the beets are tender when pierced with the tip of a knife, 40–60
minutes. Drain and, when cool enough to handle, cut off the
stem and root ends and peel off the skins. Cut a slice from the
root end of each beet so that there can be good contact on the
guiding plate. Set the straight edge of the slicing blade for a
scant ¼ inch (6 mm). Slice the beets.

Meanwhile, put the celery root in a saucepan with water to cover. Bring to a boil over high heat and boil until tender, about 15 minutes. Drain and place the celery root in a blender or food processor. Add the butter and process until smooth. Set aside.

Preheat an oven to 350°F (180°C). Line the bottom and sides of a 4$^1/_2$-by-8$^1/_2$-inch (11.5-by-21.5-cm) loaf pan with parchment (baking) paper; oil the unlined ends of the pan.

In a bowl, beat the eggs just until blended. Add all the cheeses, the onion, and the salt and pepper. Stir in the puréed celery root, mixing well. Spoon enough of the celery root mixture into the prepared pan to form an even layer about $^1/_2$ inch (12 mm) deep; you will use about one-sixth of the mixture. Top with a layer of one-third of the beet leaves. Spread with another layer of celery root, using the same amount. Top with a layer of half of the beet slices; spread with another layer of the celery root. Repeat, making 3 layers of leaves and 2 layers of sliced beets in all and ending with the celery root. Smooth the top.

Bake until browned at the edges and firm in the center, 50–60 minutes. Let rest for 10 minutes. Invert a serving plate over the pan and carefully flip the pan and plate together. Lift off the pan and peel away the paper. Cut into slices to serve. To store, wrap tightly and refrigerate for up to 3 days; bring to room temperature before serving. ✳

Grilled Pear and Gorgonzola Canapés

MAKES 16 SMALL CANAPÉS

Seek out the wonderfully rich and creamy Gorgonzola dolcelatte for these lavish open-faced sandwiches. Its smooth texture makes it easy to spread. If a firmer Gorgonzola is all that's available, you'll need to add a bit of cream to make the cheese spreadable. The pears can also be cooked under a broiler (griller), and they are especially delicious when cooked on an outdoor grill.

2 firm, ripe pears such as Anjou or Comice

6 oz (185 g) Gorgonzola cheese, at room temperature

1–2 tablespoons heavy (double) cream, or as needed

8 slices firm walnut bread, halved and crusts removed

Cut the pears in half lengthwise and remove the cores. Set the straight edge of the slicing blade for ¼ inch (6 mm) and cut 2 slices from each pear half. You will have 8 slices in all. Reserve the remaining fruit for another use.

Heat a stove-top grill pan over medium-high heat. Grill the pear slices, turning once, until lightly browned on both sides, about 4 minutes on each side. Transfer the pear slices to a plate and let cool. Cut each slice in half lengthwise.

In a small bowl, mash the Gorgonzola with a fork. Add the cream if needed to achieve a spreadable consistency. Spread the cheese in a thin layer over 1 side of each bread slice. Top each with a halved pear slice and arrange on a platter to serve. ✴

Rice-Paper Salad Rolls

MAKES 12 ROLLS; SERVES 6

6 white mushrooms, trimmed and halved lengthwise

1 cucumber, cut crosswise into 3-inch (7.5-cm) lengths

1 large carrot, peeled and cut crosswise into
3-inch (7.5-cm) lengths

1 lb (500 g) asparagus

12 rice-paper rounds, each 8½ inches (21.5 cm)
in diameter

1 bunch fresh cilantro (fresh coriander)

2 oz (60 g) bean sprouts (optional)

salt and ground pepper to taste

juice of ½ lemon

¼ cup (1¼ oz/37 g) chopped salted roasted peanuts

3 green-leaf or red-leaf lettuce leaves,
torn into 4-inch (10-cm) lengths

FOR THE DIPPING SAUCE
⅔ cup (5 fl oz/160 ml) hot water

¼ cup (2 fl oz/60 ml) Asian fish sauce

2 tablespoons lime juice

¼ cup (2 oz/60 g) sugar

2 cloves garlic, minced

1 teaspoon chile paste

24

Set the straight edge of the slicing blade for very thin slices.
Starting at the curved end, slice the mushrooms lengthwise.

Insert the ⅛-inch (3-mm) julienne blade next to the straight edge
of the slicing blade and set the guiding plate to a thickness of
⅛ inch (3 mm). Slice the cucumber pieces lengthwise into
julienne strips, rotating it as you work. Discard the seeded center
portion. Slice the carrot pieces lengthwise into julienne strips.

Snap or cut off the tough stem ends of the asparagus. Cut off
the tips and reserve for another use. Using a vegetable peeler,

peel off the tough outer skin. Slice the trimmed asparagus into julienne strips.

On a work surface, lay a sheet of wet cheesecloth (muslin) large enough to accommodate a rice-paper round, or use a sushi mat. Fill a large bowl with hot water.

Dip the edge of a rice-paper wrapper in the hot water and turn to wet completely. Place the wrapper on the cheesecloth or sushi mat, smoothing out any wrinkles. Place a row of cilantro leaves on the bottom third of the wrapper and top with four mushroom slices, about 12 strips each of the asparagus, carrots, and cucumber, and the bean sprouts, if using. Sprinkle with salt and pepper, lemon juice, and a few peanuts. Fold a piece of lettuce in half and place on top of the filling, making sure that the ingredients are evenly distributed from one end of the wrapper to the other. Press down firmly on the filling while you fold the outside edges of the wrapper over the filling. Pressing tightly, roll into a firm cylinder. Repeat to make 12 rolls.

The rolls may be made several hours ahead, covered lightly with a damp kitchen towel or wrapped with wet cheesecloth, and kept in a cool place. Do not refrigerate, or the rice-paper wrappers will toughen.

To make the sauce, in a small bowl, stir together the hot water, fish sauce, lime juice, sugar, garlic, and chile paste until the sugar dissolves.

To serve, using a sharp knife, cut each roll crosswise into 4 equal pieces. Stand the pieces on end on a platter. Serve the dipping sauce alongside. ✳

25

Cucumber and Radish Sandwiches

MAKES 12 SANDWICHES; SERVES 6

Small sandwiches are a traditional savory to serve with tea.

FOR CUCUMBER SANDWICHES

1 cucumber, peeled and cut crosswise into
3-inch (7.5-cm) lengths

6 thin slices whole-wheat (wholemeal) bread,
crusts removed

4 tablespoons (2 oz/60 g) unsalted butter,
at room temperature

salt and ground pepper to taste

FOR RADISH SANDWICHES

12 radishes, trimmed

3 thin slices firm, dark pumpernickel, crusts removed

4 teaspoons unsalted butter, at room temperature

salt to taste

To make the cucumber sandwiches, set the straight edge of
the slicing blade for very thin slices. Slice the cucumber pieces
crosswise. Cut each bread slice in half, forming rectangles.
Spread 1 teaspoon of the butter on one side of each slice and
place, buttered side up, on a work surface. Top half of the bread
slices with a row of slightly overlapping cucumber slices, sprinkle
with salt and pepper, and top with the remaining bread slices,
buttered side down.

To make the radish sandwiches, set the straight edge of the slicing blade for very thin slices. Slice the radishes crosswise. Cut
each bread slice in half, forming rectangles. Lightly butter one
side of each rectangle, top each piece with a row of overlapping
radish slices, and sprinkle with salt.

Arrange the sandwiches on a platter and serve. ✳

Smoked Salmon Bundles

MAKES 12 PIECES; SERVES 4

12 fresh chives

1 large carrot, peeled, halved lengthwise, and cut crosswise into 3-inch (7.5-cm) lengths

1 green bell pepper (capsicum), peeled

1 cucumber, cut crosswise into 3-inch (7.5-cm) lengths

salt and ground pepper to taste

juice of $1/2$ lemon

36 small fresh dill sprigs

1 or 2 thin slices smoked salmon, cut into twelve 2-inch (5-cm) squares

Bring a saucepan three-fourths full of water to a boil, blanch the chives for a few seconds, lift out and lay on paper towels to dry. Reserve the water.

Set the straight edge of the slicing blade for very thin slices. Slice the carrot pieces lengthwise. You will need 6 pieces. If not fully pliable, blanch them in the same water used for the chives.

Set the straight edge of the slicing blade for the thinnest possible slices. Holding one side of the bell pepper against the guiding plate, slice it, rotating it as you work. Trim if necessary to make 6 slices about 1 inch (2.5 cm) wide.

Insert the french-fry blade next to the straight edge of the slicing blade and set the guiding plate to a thickness of $3/8$ inch (10 mm). Slice each cucumber piece lengthwise. Discard the seeded center portion. You will need 12 sticks.

Just before assembling, season the cucumber sticks with salt, pepper, and lemon juice.

Place 3 small dill sprigs on each cucumber stick, and wrap a piece of salmon snugly around it. Wrap a strip of bell pepper over the salmon and tie with a chive. Repeat to make 5 more bundles. Then make 6 bundles, wrapped with carrot strips instead of bell pepper. Arrange on a platter and serve. ✳

Refrigerator Pickles

MAKES 2½ QT (2.5 L)

Pair these tangy, crunchy vegetables with good quality salami, or set out a bowl of them whenever you are grilling sausages. Celery, button mushrooms, and broccoli make excellent additions to the vegetable mix.

½ small cauliflower, about ½ lb (250 g), separated into florets

1 red bell pepper (capsicum)

1 turnip, peeled and halved

3 zucchini (courgettes) or yellow crookneck squashes, trimmed and cut crosswise into 2-inch (5-cm) lengths

3 large carrots, peeled and cut crosswise into 3-inch (7.5-cm) lengths

1 fennel bulb

1 red (Spanish) onion, ends trimmed

3 cloves garlic, peeled and halved lengthwise

fresh thyme sprigs (optional)

FOR THE MARINADE

1½ cups (12 fl oz/375 ml) white wine vinegar

¼ cup (2 fl oz/60 ml) canola oil

¼ cup (2 fl oz/60 ml) olive oil

5 tablespoons (2½ oz/75 g) sugar

1 tablespoon salt

¾ teaspoon ground pepper

Select a 3 qt (3 l) container with a tight-fitting lid. As the vegetables are prepared, pack them close together in the container, beginning with the cauliflower.

Insert the $^3/_{16}$-inch (5-mm) julienne blade next to the straight edge
of the slicing blade and set the guiding plate to a thickness of
$^3/_{16}$ inch (5 mm). Then, holding one side of the bell pepper
against the guiding plate, slice it, rotating it as you work. Then
slice the turnip.

Remove the julienne blade and set the serrated edge of the slicing blade for $^1/_8$ inch (3 mm). Slice the zucchini or squashes
crosswise into ruffle-cut rounds. Set the guiding plate to $^1/_6$ inch
(4 mm). Slice the carrots lengthwise into ruffle-cut slices. On a
cutting board, using a knife, cut the carrot pieces crosswise into
thirds, making ruffled squares.

Set the straight edge of the slicing blade for $^1/_4$ inch (6 mm).
Cut off the stems and feathery tops and any bruised outer stalks
from the fennel bulb. Cut the bulb in half lengthwise. Starting
with the cut edge against the guiding plate, slice the fennel
bulbs lengthwise. Then slice the onion crosswise. When all the
cut vegetables are packed into the container, tuck in the garlic
and the thyme, if using.

31

To make the marinade, in a bowl, whisk together the vinegar,
canola oil, olive oil, sugar, salt, and pepper. Pour over the vegetables; it will not cover them completely. Cover tightly and
shake gently to distribute the marinade. (Alternatively, place the
vegetables in a large bowl, add the marinade, and toss gently,
then transfer to the storage container.)

Marinate overnight and serve, or store in the refrigerator for up
to 1 month. ✳

SALADS AND SIDES

Scandinavian Cucumber Salad

SERVES 6

Freshly pickled cucumbers like these are a staple in many Swedish households, where they are traditionally served with meatballs, stews, or sandwiches.

FOR THE MARINADE

$2/3$ cup (5 fl oz/160 ml) distilled white vinegar

$1/3$ cup (3 fl oz/80 ml) water

2 tablespoons sugar

$1/2$ teaspoon salt

$1/4$ teaspoon coarsely ground pepper

2–4 tablespoons minced fresh flat-leaf (Italian) parsley

2 slender, firm cucumbers

34

To make the marinade, in a bowl, combine the vinegar, water, sugar, salt, pepper, and parsley, stirring well.

Peel the cucumbers, leaving some narrow, green lengthwise strips of peel intact for decoration. Then cut each cucumber crosswise into 3-inch (7.5-cm) lengths.

Set the straight edge of the slicing blade for very thin slices. Slice the cucumbers crosswise. Add to the marinade.

To submerge the cucumbers in the marinade, select a plate slightly smaller in diameter than the bowl and lower it onto the cucumbers. Top it with a weight, such as a can of food. Let the cucumbers marinate at room temperature for at least 4 hours or as long as overnight.

Remove the weight and the plate. Taste and adjust the seasonings, then serve with plenty of the marinade. Store in the refrigerator, covered, for up to 1 week. ✳

Celery Root Salad with Olives

SERVES 6

*The julienne blade makes quick work of producing
thin strips of celery root for this salad inspired by the
French classic* céleri-rave rémoulade.

4 cups (32 fl oz/1 l) water

2 tablespoons white wine vinegar

1 celery root (celeriac), about 1 lb (500 g)

FOR THE DRESSING

2 tablespoons mayonnaise

2 tablespoons heavy (double) cream

1 tablespoon lemon juice

$^3/_4$ teaspoon salt

ground pepper to taste

$^1/_4$ cup (1$^1/_4$ oz/37 g) green olives, pitted and
coarsely chopped

$^1/_4$ cup (1$^1/_4$ oz/37 g) black olives, pitted and
coarsely chopped

In a bowl, combine the water and vinegar. Peel the celery root
and cut it in half lengthwise. Insert the $^1/_8$-inch (3-mm) julienne
blade next to the straight edge of the slicing blade and set the
guiding plate to a thickness of $^1/_8$ inch (3 mm).

Slice the celery root into julienne strips and drop the pieces
into the vinegar water to prevent discoloration. Bring a saucepan three-fourths full of water to a boil. Drain the celery root
and add to the boiling water; blanch for 2 minutes. Drain and
rinse with cold water to stop the cooking. Drain again.

To make the dressing, in a large bowl, whisk together the mayonnaise, cream, lemon juice, salt, and pepper. Add the celery
root and toss well to coat. Taste and adjust the seasonings. Add
the olives, toss to mix, and serve. ✷

Left Bank Mushroom Salad

SERVES 6

Salads like this one are sometimes served with pâté in old-fashioned Parisian bistros. The mandoline lets you cut the thinnest possible mushrooms slices, which give this salad an intriguing texture.

FOR THE DRESSING

1 teaspoon Dijon mustard

1 teaspoon tomato paste

$1/2$ teaspoon salt

$1/4$ teaspoon ground pepper

3 tablespoons white wine vinegar

$1/2$ cup (4 fl oz/125 ml) plus 1 tablespoon olive oil

1 tablespoon heavy (double) cream

3 tablespoons snipped fresh chives

1 lb (500 g) white mushrooms, brushed clean and trimmed

lemon juice to taste

To make the dressing, in a bowl, stir together the mustard, tomato paste, salt, and pepper until smooth. Stir in the vinegar. Gradually add the olive oil, beating constantly, then stir in the cream and chives.

Set the straight edge of the slicing blade for the thinnest possible slices. Starting at the curved end, slice the mushrooms lengthwise.

Add the mushrooms to the dressing and toss to coat. Taste and add the lemon juice. Serve at once for the best texture. ✳

Shaved Fennel and Radish Salad

SERVES 6

*Try other raw vegetables prepared this way: artichokes,
mushrooms, peeled broccoli stems, celery, cucumbers, zucchini
(courgettes), kohlrabi, celery root (celeriac), turnips.
In summer, garnish with chopped fresh herbs; in winter, use
a few anchovies, capers, olives, or sun-dried tomatoes.*

1 fennel bulb

8 radishes, trimmed

1 orange

salt and ground pepper to taste

1 lemon, halved and seeded

3 tablespoons extra-virgin olive oil

Cut off the stems, feathery tops, and any bruised outer stalks
from the fennel bulb. Cut the bulb in half lengthwise. Set the
straight edge of the slicing blade for the thinnest possible slices.
Starting with the cut edge against the guiding plate, slice the
fennel halves lengthwise. Then slice the radishes.

Using a small, sharp knife, cut a slice off the top and bottom
of the orange to expose the fruit. Place the orange upright on a
cutting board. Slice off the peel in thick strips, cutting around
the contour of the orange to expose the flesh. Holding the orange
over a bowl, cut along either side of each section to free it from
the membrane, letting the sections drop into the bowl. Remove
and discard any seeds.

Arrange the fennel and radish slices and the orange sections on
a large platter. Sprinkle with salt and pepper. Squeeze half of
the lemon over the top, then drizzle with the olive oil. Taste and
adjust the seasonings, adding more lemon, olive oil, salt, or
pepper, if desired, and serve. ✳

Creamy Coleslaw

SERVES 6

*Shred the cabbage as thinly as possible for this superior version
of classic coleslaw.*

1 head green cabbage, about 2 lb (1 kg)

½ cup (4 fl oz/125 ml) mayonnaise

3 tablespoons sour cream

2 tablespoons lemon juice

1 tablespoon sugar

salt and ground pepper to taste

Cut the cabbage into quarters through the stem end. Trim core, leaving enough attached so the leaves do not separate. Set the straight edge of the slicing blade for the thinnest possible slices and slice the cabbage. Transfer to a large bowl and add cold water to cover. Cover and refrigerate for several hours.

In a small bowl, combine the mayonnaise, sour cream, lemon juice, sugar, salt, and pepper, mixing well.

Drain the cabbage well, then place in a serving bowl with the dressing and toss until evenly coated. Taste and adjust the seasonings.

Serve immediately, or cover tightly and store in the refrigerator for up to 2 days. ✳

Southern-Style Crookneck Squash

SERVES 6

*It is hard to imagine a better recipe for crookneck squash
than this one from the American South, where the summer
yield from a single squash vine can be daunting. If you
have lots of squashes, double the recipe and purée some with
stock to make a soup that is delicious hot or chilled.*

6 young, tender yellow crookneck squashes,
about 1¼ lb (625 g) total weight, ends trimmed
and halved crosswise

1 yellow onion, halved crosswise

2 tablespoons unsalted butter

½ cup (4 fl oz/125 ml) water

3 tablespoons heavy (double) cream

minced fresh flat-leaf (Italian) parsley or chives (optional)

41

Set the straight edge of the slicing blade for ⅛ inch (3 mm) and
slice the squashes and then the onion.

In a large frying pan, combine the onion and butter. Place over
medium heat, cover, and cook until the onion is soft and translucent, about 2 minutes. Add the squashes and water. Bring to
a boil over high heat, cover, reduce the heat to low, and simmer
until the squash slices are tender, 8–10 minutes.

Uncover the pan and stir in the cream. Simmer until the cooking liquid is slightly thickened, about 5 minutes.

Transfer to a warmed serving dish, garnish with parsley or
chives, if desired, and serve. ✳

Carrot Salad, Moroccan Style

SERVES 6

Aromatic from the addition of a bouquet of North African spices, these carrots complement grilled lamb or chicken.

10 large carrots, about 1 1/2 lb (750 g) total weight, peeled and cut crosswise into thirds

6 tablespoons (3 fl oz/90 ml) water

6 tablespoons (3 fl oz/90 ml) olive oil

2 cloves garlic, each cut in half lengthwise

1 1/2 teaspoons salt, or to taste

1/2 teaspoon ground black pepper, or to taste

1/4 cup (2 fl oz/60 ml) lemon juice

1 1/2 teaspoons ground cumin

3/4 teaspoon paprika

1/4 teaspoon cayenne pepper

3 tablespoons minced fresh cilantro (fresh coriander)

Insert the 3/16-inch (5-mm) julienne blade next to the straight edge of the slicing blade and set the guiding plate to a thickness of 3/16 inch (5 mm). Slice the carrot pieces lengthwise into julienne strips. You should have about 5 cups (1 1/4 lb/625 g).

To make the broth, in a large frying pan, combine the water, olive oil, garlic, 1 teaspoon of the salt, and 1/4 teaspoon of the black pepper. Add the carrots and bring to a boil over high heat. Reduce the heat to medium, cover, and cook until tender-crisp, about 5 minutes. Remove from the heat, uncover, and let cool in the broth.

Drain the cooled carrots and place in a bowl. Add the lemon juice, cumin, paprika, cayenne pepper, and the remaining salt and black pepper. Toss well, then taste and adjust the seasonings. Sprinkle with the cilantro and serve at once. ✳

Herbed Zucchini Sauté

SERVES 6

Thin slices of zucchini, sautéed quickly, retain their fresh flavor.
Serve as an accompaniment to chicken, pork chops, or roasts.

6 zucchini (courgettes), about 1½ lb (750 g)
total weight, ends trimmed and halved crosswise

2 tablespoons olive oil

1 clove garlic, chopped

2 tablespoons chopped fresh flat-leaf (Italian) parsley or
chives or 1 tablespoon chopped fresh oregano

2 tablespoons grated Parmesan cheese

Set the straight edge of the slicing blade for the thinnest possible slices and slice all of the zucchini crosswise.

In a large frying pan over medium-high heat, warm the olive oil. Add the zucchini and cook, stirring, until limp, about 5 minutes. Push the zucchini to one side of the pan and add the garlic to the cleared space. Cook, stirring, until the garlic is softened, about 1 minute. Add the parsley, chives, or oregano and toss with the garlic and zucchini to mix.

Transfer to a warmed serving dish, sprinkle with the Parmesan cheese, and serve. ✳

Sautéed Shaved Asparagus with Asparagus Tips

SERVES 6

Here, butter-steamed shavings of the asparagus stalks and a garnish of the tender tips offer two aspects of the spring vegetable on the same plate. Select thick asparagus spears, as they are easier to slice on the mandoline than thin ones. Serve as a perfect companion to grilled salmon.

3 lb (1.5 kg) asparagus

4 tablespoons (2 oz/60 g) unsalted butter

3 tablespoons water

$1/2$ teaspoon salt, plus salt to taste

grated zest of $1/2$ lemon

ground pepper to taste

1 tablespoon lemon juice

45

Cut off the tips from the asparagus and reserve. Break off the tough ends of the asparagus stalks and discard. Using a vegetable peeler, peel off the thin outer skin from the tender stalk portions. Set the straight edge of the slicing blade for the thinnest possible slices and slice the asparagus stalks lengthwise.

Fill a saucepan three-fourths full of salted water and bring to a boil. Add the asparagus tips and cook until just tender, about 4 minutes. Drain well and pat dry with a kitchen towel.

In a large frying pan, combine the sliced asparagus, 2 tablespoons of the butter, the water, the $1/2$ teaspoon salt, and the lemon zest. Cover, place over high heat, and bring to a boil. Cook until just tender, about 2 minutes. If any liquid remains, cook uncovered to evaporate it. Add salt and pepper to taste. Keep warm. In a small pan, melt the remaining 2 tablespoons butter. Transfer the asparagus tips to a warmed serving bowl, pour the melted butter and the lemon juice over them, and season with salt. Push the tips to the sides of the bowl, place the asparagus shavings in the middle, and serve at once. ✳

Pommes Maxim's

SERVES 6

At the legendary restaurant Maxim's in Paris,
golden potato cakes like this one are presented at the table
in gleaming copper pans. This makes a terrific side dish
for a roast chicken.

4 tablespoons (2 oz/60 g) unsalted butter

2 russet potatoes, about 1 lb (500 g) total weight,
peeled, ends trimmed, and halved crosswise

$^3/_4$ teaspoon salt

$^1/_4$ teaspoon ground pepper

coarse salt to taste (optional)

Preheat an oven to 425°F (220°C). Select a large baking dish, such as a 14-inch (35-cm) oval enameled cast-iron gratin dish. Grease the dish with 1 tablespoon of the butter.

Have ready a bowl full of cold water. Set the straight edge of the slicing blade for $^1/_8$ inch (3 mm) and slice the potatoes crosswise. Transfer the slices to the water as soon as they are cut. Let soak for a few minutes, then drain the potatoes and pat dry with paper towels.

Arrange a layer of overlapping potato slices, using about one-third of them, in the prepared baking dish. Sprinkle with some of the salt and pepper. Cut the remaining 3 tablespoons butter into bits and dot the surface with one-third of it. Repeat with the remaining potatoes, butter, salt and pepper to make 3 layers; all the layers combined should not stand more than $^1/_2$ inch (12 mm) high.

Bake until the surface turns light golden brown and is thoroughly crisp, 20–25 minutes. Sprinkle with coarse salt, if desired, and serve at once. ✶

Jicama in Citrus Dressing

*Crunchy, bland jicama gets a lift from orange and lime juices.
Include plenty of dressing with each serving.*

2 jicamas, about 1 lb (500 g) total weight,
peeled and halved lengthwise

FOR THE DRESSING

5 tablespoons (2½ fl oz/75 ml) lime juice

3 tablespoons orange juice

1 tablespoon honey

³/₄ teaspoon salt

2 teaspoons chopped fresh cilantro (fresh coriander)

48

Insert the ³/₁₆-inch (5-mm) julienne blade next to the straight
edge of the slicing blade and set the guiding plate to a thickness
of ³/₁₆ inch (5 mm). Place the cut side of the jicama against the
guiding plate and cut into julienne strips. Place in a serving bowl.

To make the dressing, in a small bowl, stir together the lime
juice, orange juice, honey, and salt; mix well to dissolve the
honey completely. Pour the dressing over the jicama, add the
cilantro, and toss well. Serve at once in shallow bowls. ✳

Sautéed Noodle-Cut Cucumbers

SERVES 6

French cooks often serve sautéed cucumbers as a side dish.
They have a delightful tender-crisp texture when cooked and taste
marvelously of whatever seasonings you add to them.

6 cucumbers, peeled and cut in half crosswise

2$\frac{1}{2}$ teaspoons salt

2 tablespoons olive oil

ground pepper to taste

2 teaspoons capers or to taste, well rinsed

2 teaspoons lemon juice, or to taste

1 tablespoon chopped fresh flat-leaf (Italian) parsley

Insert the $\frac{3}{16}$-inch (5-mm) julienne blade next to the straight
edge of the slicing blade and set the guiding plate to a thickness
of $\frac{3}{16}$ inch (5 mm). Slice each cucumber piece lengthwise into
julienne strips, rotating it as you work. Discard the seeded
center portion. As the strips are cut, layer them in a colander,
sprinkling the layers with 2 teaspoons of the salt. Let stand for
30 minutes, then rinse with cold water. Transfer to a large
kitchen towel, fold in the sides, roll up, and press gently to remove excess water.

49

In a large sauté pan over medium-high heat, warm the olive oil.
Heat until a strip of cucumber dropped into it sizzles upon contact. Then add all the cucumbers to the pan and sauté, stirring
occasionally, until translucent and glossy, about 2 minutes.
Add the remaining $\frac{1}{2}$ teaspoon salt, the pepper, the capers, the
lemon juice, and the parsley. Toss together gently and transfer
to a warmed serving bowl. Serve at once. ✳

Yams with Ginger and Lemon

SERVES 6

*This tangy version of candied yams, with its ruffle-cut slices,
tastes divine with spicy sausages or barbecued turkey. If you prefer
a browner top, use a flameproof baking dish and slip it
under the broiler (griller) for a minute or so after it is baked.*

4 yams such as garnet or Diane, about 2 lb (1 kg) total
weight, peeled and cut crosswise into 3-inch (7.5-cm) pieces

1 piece fresh ginger, about 2 inches (5 cm) long, sliced

2 teaspoons salt

1/4 cup (3 oz/90 g) light molasses

1/4 cup (2 oz/60 g) sugar

1 tablespoon lemon juice

1/4 teaspoon ground nutmeg

1/4 teaspoon ground pepper

3 tablespoons unsalted butter, cut into small bits

Preheat an oven to 400°F (200°C). Butter a 2-qt (2-l) baking
dish. Set the serrated edge of the slicing blade for 3/8 inch
(10 mm) and slice the yams crosswise.

In a large frying pan, combine the sliced yams, ginger, and salt
with water to cover. Bring to a boil over high heat, reduce the
heat to medium, and boil gently until fork tender, 10–15 minutes. Drain, discarding the ginger.

Place the yam slices in the prepared dish, overlapping them
slightly. In a small bowl, stir together the molasses, sugar, and
lemon juice. Pour evenly over the yams. Dust the top evenly
with the nutmeg and pepper, then dot with the butter.

Bake until the edges of the yam slices turn a darker shade of
orange, 20–30 minutes. Serve at once, directly from the dish,
distributing any juices evenly among the portions. ✳

MAIN COURSES

Leek and Potato Pizza

SERVES 6

2 thick slices bacon, about 2 oz (60 g) total weight,
cut into pieces $\frac{1}{2}$ inch (12 mm) wide

1 large leek, about $\frac{1}{2}$ lb (250 g), white and
tender light green portion only

1 teaspoon olive oil

1 small russet potato, about $\frac{1}{4}$ lb (125 g), unpeeled,
ends trimmed and halved crosswise

1 tablespoon cornmeal

1 lb (500 g) frozen bread dough, thawed

6 oz (185 g) mozzarella cheese, shredded

3 oz (90 g) fontina cheese, shredded

15 green olives, pitted and coarsely chopped

In a small frying pan over medium-low heat, fry the bacon to render the fat without fully cooking the bacon, about 10 minutes. Transfer to paper towels to drain.

Meanwhile, set the straight edge of the slicing blade for $\frac{3}{8}$ inch (10 mm). Slice the leek. In a small frying pan over medium-low heat, combine the leek and the olive oil, cover, and cook until softened, about 5 minutes; do not allow to brown.

Set the straight edge of the slicing blade for the thinnest possible slices and slice the potato.

Preheat an oven to 425°F (220°C). Spray a 15-inch (38-cm) pizza pan or large baking sheet with nonstick cooking spray and dust with the cornmeal.

Roll out the dough into a round $\frac{1}{4}$ inch (6 mm) thick. Transfer to the prepared pan and pinch the edges to form a rim. Sprinkle all but about 1 cup (4 oz/125 g) of the cheeses over the dough. Distribute the bacon, leek, potato slices, and olives on top and sprinkle with the remaining cheese.

Bake until the top is lightly browned, about 25 minutes. Remove from the oven, cut into wedges, and serve. ✱

Zucchini Moussaka

SERVES 8

*Slices of eggplant (aubergine) or potato can be used
instead of zucchini. Cucumber slices chilled in garlicky yogurt
are a nice accompaniment.*

FOR THE MEAT SAUCE

1 tablespoon unsalted butter

1 yellow onion, chopped

2 lb (1 kg) ground (minced) lamb or beef

1 cup (8 fl oz/250 ml) tomato sauce

$^3/_4$ cup (6 fl oz/180 ml) water

2 tablespoons minced fresh flat-leaf (Italian) parsley

FOR THE VEGETABLE LAYER

6 zucchini (courgettes), trimmed to 5 inches (13 cm)
and halved lengthwise

3 tablespoons vegetable oil

FOR THE BÉCHAMEL SAUCE

6 tablespoons (3 oz/90 g) unsalted butter

$^1/_4$ cup (1 $^1/_2$ oz/45 g) plus 1 tablespoon
all-purpose (plain) flour

$^1/_4$ teaspoon salt

3 cups (24 fl oz/750 ml) milk

$^1/_2$ cup (2 oz/60 g) grated Parmesan cheese

To make the meat sauce, in a large frying pan over medium
heat, combine the butter and onion and cook, stirring, until
the onion softens and begins to color, about 3 minutes. Add
the ground meat and cook, stirring constantly, until the meat
is crumbly and no longer pink, about 10 minutes. Stir in the
tomato sauce and water and bring to a boil. Reduce the heat
to low and simmer, uncovered, until most of the liquid has
evaporated, about 5 minutes. Remove from the heat and, using
a spoon, skim off as much of the fat as possible. Stir in the
parsley and set aside.

To make the vegetable layer, set the straight edge of the slicing blade for $1/4$ inch (6 mm) and cut the zucchini lengthwise into several long slices, discarding the end slices. You will need 18 fairly uniform slices in all. Pat the slices dry with paper towels.

In a large frying pan over medium-high heat, warm the oil. Working in batches, add the zucchini slices and fry, turning once, until pale gold, about 5 minutes on each side. Transfer to paper towels to drain.

Preheat an oven to 375°F (190°C). Oil a 9-by-13-inch (23-by-33-cm) baking dish.

To make the béchamel sauce, in a heavy saucepan over medium heat, melt the butter. Whisk in the flour and salt and cook, stirring constantly with the whisk, for about 3 minutes; do not brown. Remove from the heat and gradually whisk in the milk. Return to medium heat and cook, whisking constantly, until the sauce is the consistency of heavy (double) cream, about 10 minutes. Remove from the heat.

57

Spread about one-fourth of the meat sauce in a thin layer on the bottom of the prepared dish. Arrange 6 zucchini slices in a single layer on top of the sauce. Sprinkle with 2 tablespoons of the Parmesan cheese. Repeat the layers twice. Spread the remaining meat sauce on top. Pour the béchamel sauce evenly over the top and sprinkle with the remaining 2 tablespoons Parmesan cheese.

Bake until the edges are browned and the topping is set, 40–50 minutes. Remove from the oven and let rest for at least 10 minutes before cutting into squares. Serve warm. ✽

Pasta with Slow-Cooked Onions

SERVES 6

1 1/2 lb (750 g) yellow onions, halved crosswise

2 tablespoons unsalted butter

2 tablespoons olive oil

3 tablespoons water

1 tablespoon balsamic vinegar

1 teaspoon salt

1/2 teaspoon ground pepper

2 tablespoons minced fresh flat-leaf (Italian) parsley

1 1/4 lb (625 g) short dried pasta such as penne

lemon juice to taste

1/4 cup (1/2 oz/15 g) fresh bread crumbs, lightly toasted

1/4 cup (1 1/4 oz/37 g) hazelnuts (filberts), lightly toasted
and coarsely chopped

Set the straight edge of the slicing blade for very thin slices and
slice the onions.

In a large frying pan over low heat, combine the butter, olive
oil, and onions. Cover and cook until dark golden and very soft,
about 1 hour. Raise the heat to medium, uncover, and cook until
the liquid evaporates, about 10 minutes. Add the water, vinegar,
salt, and pepper and raise the heat to medium-high. Cook, stirring, until the liquid evaporates again, about 5 minutes. Remove
from the heat and stir in the parsley.

Meanwhile, bring a large pot three-fourths full of salted water
to a boil. Add the pasta, stir, and cook until al dente (tender but
firm to the bite), about 12 minutes or according to the package
directions. Drain and toss with the sauce and lemon juice. Divide among warmed individual bowls. Sprinkle with the bread
crumbs and nuts and serve. ✳

Eggplant Lasagne

SERVES 6

FOR THE TOMATO SAUCE

2 tablespoons unsalted butter

2 tablespoons vegetable oil

2 yellow onions, chopped

1 1/2 cups (9 oz/280 g) canned tomatoes,
chopped, with their juices

1 teaspoon salt

1/4 teaspoon red pepper flakes

2 eggplants (aubergines), about 2 lb (1 kg) total weight

1/2 lb (250 g) lasagne noodles

1/4 cup (1 oz/30 g) pine nuts

3 tablespoons butter

2 teaspoons cornstarch (cornflour)

1 1/2 cups (12 fl oz/375 ml) milk

3 egg yolks

1 whole egg

1 cup (8 oz/250 g) ricotta cheese, passed through a sieve

3 tablespoons grated Parmesan cheese

To make the tomato sauce, in a saucepan over medium heat, combine the butter, oil, and onions. Cook, stirring, until softened, about 10 minutes. Add the tomatoes and their juice, salt, and red pepper flakes, reduce the heat to low, and simmer until the oil separates from the sauce, about 25 minutes.

Meanwhile, preheat an oven to 375°F (190°C). Line 2 large baking sheets with aluminum foil, dull side up. Spray the foil lightly with nonstick cooking spray.

Peel the eggplants and trim the tops and bottoms. Cut in half lengthwise. Set the straight edge of the slicing blade for 1/4 inch (6 mm) and slice the eggplant lengthwise. Place in a single layer on the prepared baking sheets and spray with nonstick cooking spray. Bake until the undersides are browned, 12–15 minutes. Remove from the oven and set aside.

Reduce the oven temperature to 325°F (165°C). Spray a 9-by-13-inch (23-by-33-cm) baking pan with nonstick cooking spray.

In a large pot three-fourths full of boiling salted water, cook the noodles until almost tender, 8–12 minutes or according to package directions. Drain, immerse in cold water, and drain again. Lay the noodles flat on a kitchen towel and pat dry.

In a small, dry frying pan over medium heat, toast the pine nuts, shaking the pan constantly, until aromatic and lightly browned, about 4 minutes. Transfer to a dish and set aside.

Meanwhile, in a heavy saucepan over medium heat, melt the butter. Stir in the cornstarch and cook, stirring, until bubbling, about 2 minutes. Stir in the milk and cook, stirring constantly, until smooth, about 3 minutes. In a small bowl, whisk together the egg yolks and whole egg. Whisk a few spoonfuls of hot sauce into the eggs, then add the egg mixture to the sauce in the pan and cook, stirring, until slightly thickened, about 4 minutes. Remove from the heat and stir in the ricotta.

61

Place one-fourth of the noodles in a single layer in the prepared pan. Top with one-third of the tomato sauce, one-third of the eggplant slices, one-third of the pine nuts, and 1 tablespoon of the Parmesan cheese. Repeat all the layers twice, then top with the remaining noodles. Pour the ricotta mixture over the top.

Bake until golden brown, about 40 minutes. Remove from the oven and let rest for at least 30 minutes. Serve warm. ✳

Baked Omelet with Potatoes, Leeks, Ham, and Peas

SERVES 6

2 leeks, including 2 inches (5 cm) of green, thinly sliced

4 tablespoons (2 fl oz/60 ml) olive oil

1/2 cup (2 1/2 oz/75 g) frozen peas

2 russet potatoes, about 1 lb (500 g) total weight,
peeled, ends trimmed, and halved crosswise

8 eggs

3/4 cup (4 1/2 oz/140 g) diced ham

1 teaspoon salt

ground pepper to taste

Preheat an oven to 325°F (165°C). Generously oil a 10-inch (25-cm) round baking dish.

In a frying pan over medium heat, combine the leeks and 2 tablespoons of the oil. Cover and cook until softened, about 7 minutes. Transfer to a plate. In a small bowl, cover the peas with warm water and let stand for 3 minutes; drain.

Set the straight edge of the slicing blade for 1/8 inch (3 mm) and slice the potatoes crosswise. Warm the remaining 2 tablespoons oil in the frying pan over medium heat. Add the potatoes and cook, stirring occasionally, until tender but not browned, about 15 minutes. Using a slotted spoon, transfer to a plate to cool.

In a large bowl, beat the eggs just until blended. Add the leeks, peas, potatoes, ham, salt, and pepper; mix lightly. Pour into the prepared baking dish.

Bake until golden brown and set, 30–40 minutes. Let cool for 20 minutes, then invert onto a serving plate. Cut the omelet into wedges and serve. ✳

Potato and Leek Soup with Butternut Squash Gratin

SERVES 6

A slice of savory squash gratin brings a contrast of color, texture, and flavor to a bowl of potato-leek soup. Serve with a chicory (curly endive) salad for a satisfying fall meal.

3 leeks, white parts only, cut into 3-inch (7.5-cm) lengths

1 small yellow onion, halved crosswise

3 tablespoons unsalted butter

2 russet potatoes, about 1 lb (500 g) total weight, peeled and cut into chunks

1 $^3/_4$ teaspoons salt

ground black pepper to taste

pinch of cayenne pepper

6 cups (48 fl oz/1.5 l) water

6 tablespoons ($^3/_4$ oz/20 g) coarse fresh bread crumbs

1 butternut squash, about 2 lbs (1 kg), halved lengthwise and seeds and fibers discarded

2 tablespoons vegetable oil

64

Set the straight edge of the slicing blade for very thin slices and slice the leeks and the onion.

In a large saucepan over medium-low heat, combine 2 tablespoons of the butter, the leeks, and the onion. Cover and cook until wilted, about 5 minutes. Add the potatoes and cook, covered, until softened, about 10 minutes. Add 1 teaspoon of the salt, the $^1/_4$ teaspoon black pepper, cayenne, and water. Increase the heat to medium-high and bring to a gentle boil, cover partially, and cook until very tender, about 30 minutes. Remove from the heat and let cool slightly, then purée in a blender, working in batches if necessary. Return to a clean saucepan.

Meanwhile, preheat an oven to 350°F (180°C). Spread the bread crumbs in a small pan and toast in the oven until lightly browned, about 8 minutes. Remove from the oven and set aside. Raise the oven temperature to 400°F (200°C).

Cut the squash into 8 uniform pieces and peel them. Set the straight edge of the slicing blade for ¹/₈ inch (3 mm) and slice the squash.

Put the squash slices in a large baking dish and toss with 1 table-spoon of the oil. Cover and bake until just barely tender, about 15 minutes. Spread the remaining 1 tablespoon oil in a 14-inch (35-cm) oval gratin dish or in a 9-by-13-inch (23-by-33-cm) baking pan. Place the precooked squash slices, curved edges uppermost, in overlapping rows in the dish. Sprinkle with the remaining ³/₄ teaspoon salt and a few grindings of black pepper. Cut the remaining 1 tablespoon butter into bits and use to dot the surface. Dust with the toasted bread crumbs.

Bake, uncovered, until the squash is browned at the edges, about 15 minutes.

Reheat the soup to serving temperature. Ladle into 6 large, shallow bowls, dividing it evenly. Divide the gratin into 6 equal pieces and place a piece in each bowl. Serve at once. ✳

Warm Cabbage Salad with Smoked Chicken and Walnuts

SERVES 6

The vibrant color of the cabbage sets off the smoked chicken breast in this main-course salad. Leftover roast chicken or pork tenderloin can be used in place of the smoked chicken. This easy-to-assemble salad is a good choice for a casual lunch or late-night supper.

$\frac{1}{2}$ cup (2 oz/60 g) walnuts

I red cabbage, quartered lengthwise and cored

I smoked chicken breast, about $\frac{3}{4}$ lb (375 g)

$\frac{1}{4}$ cup (2 fl oz/60 ml) vegetable oil

6 green (spring) onions, cut on the diagonal into $\frac{1}{2}$-inch (12-mm) pieces

6 tablespoons (3 fl oz/90 ml) red wine vinegar

3 tablespoons sugar

I teaspoon salt

$\frac{1}{2}$ teaspoon ground pepper

lemon juice to taste, if needed

Preheat an oven to 275°F (135°C). Spread the walnuts on a baking sheet and place in the oven until lightly toasted and fragrant, about 10 minutes. Remove the nuts from the oven and set aside to cool.

Set the straight edge of the slicing blade for $\frac{1}{4}$ inch (6 mm) and slice the cabbage quarters lengthwise to make long shreds. Set aside. Using a knife, slice the chicken meat off the bone into strips about 1 by $1\frac{1}{2}$ inches (2.5 by 4 cm) and set aside.

In a large frying pan over medium heat, warm the vegetable oil. Add the green onions and cook, stirring, until softened, about 3 minutes. Add the cabbage in 2 batches, allowing the first batch to soften slightly and collapse before adding the remainder. (Most pans will not be large enough to contain all the raw

(continued on next page)

Warm Cabbage Salad with
Smoked Chicken and Walnuts
(continued from previous page)

cabbage at once.) Cook, stirring occasionally, until tender, about 20 minutes.

Meanwhile, in a small bowl, stir together the vinegar, sugar, salt, and pepper. When the cabbage is tender, pour the vinegar mixture into the pan. Toss thoroughly with the cabbage and cook until warmed through, 3–5 minutes. Taste and add lemon juice, if needed.

Transfer the cabbage to a warmed large platter. Arrange the chicken strips down the center and garnish with the walnuts. Serve warm. ✳

Country Potato-and-Sausage Gratin

SERVES 6

*Sausage and cheese turn an ordinary potato gratin into
a satisfying main course. The mandoline makes quick work
of slicing the potatoes and, because they are uniformly cut,
the potatoes cook more evenly.*

4 russet potatoes, about 2 lb (1 kg) total weight,
peeled, ends trimmed, and halved crosswise

2 spicy smoked sausages such as pepperoni,
about ¹/₂ lb (250 g) total weight

1 cup (8 fl oz/250 ml) low-sodium beef or chicken broth

salt and ground pepper to taste

³/₄ cup (3 oz/90 g) shredded Gruyère, Muenster,
or other mild melting cheese

69

Preheat an oven to 350°F (180°C). Butter a large baking dish
such as a 14-inch (35-cm) oval gratin dish.

Set the straight edge of the slicing blade for ¹/₈ inch (3 mm) and
slice the potatoes crosswise. Set aside. Using a knife, thinly slice
the sausages and set aside. In a small saucepan, bring the broth
to a boil and keep warm.

Arrange one-third of the potato slices in an even layer in the
prepared dish. Sprinkle with salt and a few grindings of pepper.
Scatter one-third of the cheese over the potatoes, then scatter
one-third of the sausage slices over the cheese. Repeat the layers
twice, ending with a layer of cheese. Slowly pour the hot broth
into the gratin dish along one side.

Bake until the potatoes are tender when pierced with a fork and
the edges of the gratin are browned, 50–60 minutes. Serve hot
directly from the dish. ✳

Braised Pork Chops with Root Vegetable Julienne

SERVES 6

Sweet and earthy root vegetables are a classic accompaniment to pork, and cutting them into thin strips is easy when you use the julienne blade of the mandoline. Serve these chops with a bowl of buttery polenta, a crisp green salad, and a bottle of red wine on a night when the wind outside is roaring.

2 large carrots, peeled and cut crosswise
into 3-inch (7.5-cm) lengths

3 turnips, about $1/2$ lb (250 g) total weight,
peeled and halved lengthwise

2 rutabagas, about $1/2$ lb (250 g) total weight,
peeled and halved lengthwise

2 celery stalks, cut crosswise into 3-inch
(7.5-cm) lengths

3 tablespoons corn oil

6 pork chops, about 5 oz (155 g) each

1 clove garlic, halved lengthwise

$3/4$ cup (6 fl oz/180 ml) chicken broth

1 fresh thyme sprig or $1/4$ teaspoon dried thyme

1 teaspoon salt

$1/4$ teaspoon ground pepper

2 tablespoons red wine vinegar

70

Insert the $3/16$-inch (5-mm) julienne blade next to the straight edge of the slicing blade and set the guiding plate to a thickness of $3/16$ inch (5 mm). Cut the carrots lengthwise into julienne strips. Then cut the turnips and rutabagas lengthwise into julienne strips. With the rounded surface against the guiding plate, cut the celery lengthwise into julienne strips.

In a large frying pan over medium-high heat, warm the oil. Add the julienned vegetables and cook, stirring occasionally, until just beginning to brown, about 5 minutes. Using a slotted spoon, remove the vegetables from the pan and set aside. Working in batches, if necessary, add the pork chops and brown, turning once, about 4 minutes on each side. When all the chops are browned, overlap them as necessary to fit into the pan. Add the garlic, broth, thyme, salt, and pepper. Bring to a boil, reduce the heat to low, cover, and simmer, turning once, until firm to the touch and still slightly pink inside, about 45 minutes.

Transfer the chops to a warmed serving platter and keep warm. Skim off any fat from the pan juices. Add the julienned vegetables to the juices in the pan, cover, and simmer over medium heat until tender, about 5 minutes. Using a slotted spoon, transfer the vegetables to the serving platter. Add the vinegar to the pan juices, raise the heat to high, and cook until the juices are thickened and reduced to about $1/4$ cup (2 fl oz/60 ml), about 2 minutes. Spoon the reduced cooking juices over the chops and vegetables and serve. ✷

Zucchini Pasta with Tomato Sauce

SERVES 6

Zucchini can be cut into strips that resemble noodles and tossed with a quick-cooking tomato sauce for a simple late-night supper.

8 zucchini (courgettes), about 2½ lb (1.25 kg) total weight, trimmed to pieces 7–10 inches (18–25 cm) long

2 teaspoons salt

½ lb (250 g) linguine, fedelini, or other long, thin pasta

FOR THE TOMATO SAUCE

¼ cup (2 fl oz/60 ml) olive oil

6 plum (Roma) tomatoes, about 1 lb (500 g) total weight, seeded and cut into large dice

3 cloves garlic, minced

6 tablespoons (½ oz/15 g) minced fresh flat-leaf (Italian) parsley

½ teaspoon red pepper flakes

salt and ground black pepper to taste

¼ cup (1 oz/30 g) grated Parmesan cheese

73

Insert the ³/₁₆-inch (5-mm) julienne blade next to the straight edge of the slicing blade and set the guiding plate to a thickness of ³/₁₆ inch (5 mm). Cut each zucchini into julienne strips, rotating it as you work. Discard the seeded center portion. Place in a colander, sprinkle with the salt, and let drain for 30 minutes.

Cook the pasta in a large pot three-fourths full of boiling salted water until tender but firm to the bite, about 6 minutes or according to package directions. About 2 minutes before the pasta is done, add the zucchini. Drain and transfer to a serving bowl.

Meanwhile, in a frying pan over medium heat, warm the olive oil. Add the tomatoes and cook until heated through, about 2 minutes. Add the garlic and cook until fragrant, about 2 minutes. Stir in the parsley, red pepper flakes, salt, and black pepper. Add to the pasta and toss to combine. Sprinkle with the cheese and serve. ✳

Asian Chicken Noodle Soup

SERVES 6

2 skinless, boneless chicken breast halves,
about 10 oz (315 g) each

6 cups (48 fl oz/1.5 l) chicken broth

6 broccoli stalks, about 2 lb (1 kg) total weight

2 yellow bell peppers (capsicums)

1 package (14 oz/440 g) rice vermicelli noodles

1 tablespoon soy sauce

12 fresh cilantro (fresh coriander) sprigs

2 green (spring) onions, chopped

1 jalapeño chile, seeded and chopped

Asian chile sauce

Asian fish sauce

In a saucepan, combine the chicken and enough of the broth to cover by 1 inch (2.5 cm). Bring to a boil over medium-high heat, reduce the heat to low, and simmer until the chicken is cooked through, 10–12 minutes. Lift out with a slotted spoon. Reserve the broth, recombining it with the remaining broth. Cut the chicken into strips on the diagonal; reserve.

Cut the florets from the broccoli and reserve for another use. Trim the tough ends from the stalks, then, using a vegetable peeler, peel off the tough outer skin. Insert the $^3/_{16}$-inch (5-mm) julienne blade next to the straight edge of the slicing blade and set the guiding plate to $^3/_{16}$ inch (5 mm). Slice the stalks into strips. Then slice each bell pepper, rotating it as you work.

In a large pot three-fourths full of boiling water, cook the vermicelli until tender, 6–8 minutes. Drain the noodles, rinse with cold water, and reserve.

Bring the broth to a boil and add the noodles. As soon as the broth returns to a boil, add the broccoli and pepper strips and cook until barely tender, about 2 minutes. Add the chicken and soy sauce and remove from the heat.

Serve in warmed bowls. Pass the cilantro, green onions, chopped chile, chile sauce, and fish sauce at the table. ✳

Vegetables in Cashew Curry Sauce

SERVES 6

Serve the subtly spiced curry with basmati rice flecked with bits of blanched carrots. Almonds can be used in place of the cashews and cauliflower florets can stand in for the green beans.

FOR THE GINGER PASTE

5 tablespoons (2 oz/60 g) cashews

3 cloves garlic, coarsely chopped

1 piece fresh ginger, about 1 inch (2.5 cm) long, peeled and coarsely chopped

1–3 fresh green chiles such as jalapeño or serrano, sliced

$^3/_4$ cup (6 fl oz/180 ml) water

FOR THE VEGETABLE CURRY

4 red potatoes, about 1 lb (500 g) total weight, peeled and halved crosswise

3 kohlrabi or turnips, about 1 lb (500 g) total weight, peeled and cut crosswise

1 can (14 fl oz/430 ml) coconut milk

$^1/_4$ cup (2 fl oz/60 ml) canola or other mild vegetable oil

10 green cardamom pods

1 cinnamon stick

8 whole cloves

2 yellow onions, finely chopped

$^3/_4$ lb (375 g) green beans, trimmed and cut into 2-inch (5-cm) pieces

2 teaspoons salt

To make the ginger paste, in a blender, combine the cashews, garlic, ginger, and chiles. Blend for a few seconds to chop. Add the water and blend to form a smooth paste, about 2 minutes. Set aside.

To make the curry, insert the $^3/_8$-inch (10-mm) french-fry blade next to the straight edge of the slicing blade and set the guiding plate to a thickness of $^3/_8$ inch (10 mm). Place the potatoes, cut side down, on the guiding plate and cut into sticks. Then cut the kohlrabi or turnips in the same way. Pour the coconut milk into a measuring pitcher and add water as needed to measure 2 cups (16 fl oz/500 ml).

In a large frying pan over medium heat, warm the oil. Add the cardamom pods, cinnamon stick, and cloves and stir for a few seconds. Add the onions and cook, stirring constantly, until uniformly golden brown, about 10 minutes. Add the ginger paste and cook, stirring, until golden, 3–4 minutes. Add the potatoes, kohlrabi or turnips, and green beans and stir together gently, distributing the fried mixture evenly. Add the coconut milk and the salt, reduce the heat to low, cover, and simmer until the vegetables are tender and the sauce is thick and creamy, 20–25 minutes. Remove and discard the cardomom pods, cinnamon stick, and cloves. (The curry can be made up to 2 days in advance, covered, and refrigerated. Reheat gently before serving.)

77

Divide among 6 warmed individual plates and serve at once. ✴

DESSERTS

Hasty Charlottes

SERVES 6

Sautéed apple slices tossed with bread cubes are assembled more quickly than the classic apple charlotte (puréed apples in a bread-lined mold), but none of the seductive flavors of the original are lost.

6 green cooking apples such as Granny Smith, about 1 lb (500 g) total weight, quartered and cored

7 tablespoons (3½ oz/105 g) unsalted butter

6 oz (185 g) firm white bread, crusts removed, thinly sliced, and cut into 1-inch (2.5-cm) squares (about 2 cups/4 oz/125 g)

6 tablespoons (3 oz/90 g) sugar

¼ cup (2 fl oz/60 ml) lemon juice

1 tablespoon dark rum

crème fraîche for serving

Preheat an oven to 400°F (200°C). Generously butter six ¾-cup (6–fl oz/180-ml) ramekins or custard cups.

Set the straight edge of the slicing blade for ¼ inch (6 mm) and slice the apples. In a large frying pan over medium heat, melt 6 tablespoons (3 oz/90 g) of the butter. Add the apple slices and cook, stirring, until they soften and change color, about 10 minutes. Add the bread cubes and toss for 1–2 minutes. Remove from the heat and stir in the sugar, lemon juice, and rum, mixing well. Divide the mixture evenly among the molds, pressing it in gently if necessary and leveling the tops. Cut the remaining 1 tablespoon butter into bits and use to dot the tops.

Bake until golden brown and bubbling, about 40 minutes. Let cool for about 5 minutes before unmolding onto serving plates. Serve warm. Pass the crème fraîche at the table. ✳

Melon Sorbet Express

SERVES 6

When summer melons are at their peak, use them to make this mock sorbet. Its intriguing frosty texture makes for a refreshing dessert.

FOR THE LIME-RUM SYRUP

¼ cup (2 oz/60 g) sugar

2 tablespoons water

2 tablespoons lime juice or orange juice

2 tablespoons light rum

½ ripe honeydew melon or cantaloupe, seeded, peeled, and cut into wedges 1½ inches (4 cm) wide

To make the syrup, in a small saucepan over high heat, bring the sugar and water to a boil, stirring to dissolve the sugar. Reduce the heat to medium and simmer until the sugar is dissolved, about 5 minutes. Remove from the heat and stir in the lime juice and rum. Let cool completely.

In a metal pan, arrange the melon wedges in a single layer. Freeze until firm but not icy, about 30 minutes. The melon should not be frozen so hard that it cannot be sliced easily.

Just before serving, cut the melon wedges into 1½-inch (4-cm) lengths. Set the straight edge of the slicing blade for ⅛ inch (3 mm). Slice the melon wedges. Place them in small individual bowls, pour the syrup over the top, and serve. ✳

Nectarine Upside-Down Cake

SERVES 6–8

You can slice fresh nectarines quickly on the mandoline without the messy task of pitting them; just slice until you reach the pit, then rotate the fruit.

4 or 5 nectarines, unpeeled

2 tablespoons firmly packed golden brown sugar

2 eggs, at room temperature

1 cup (8 oz/250 g) granulated sugar

1 cup (5 oz/155 g) all-purpose (plain) flour

1/2 cup (4 oz/125 g) unsalted butter, melted

1 teaspoon vanilla extract (essence)

Preheat an oven to 350°F (180°C). Generously butter a 9-inch (23-cm) round cake pan.

Set the straight edge of the slicing blade for 1/4 inch (6 mm) and cut a few lengthwise slices from a nectarine, until you reach the pit. Rotate the fruit by one-third, so you have a fresh section to work with, and continue slicing. Rotate one more time to remove all the sliceable flesh. Repeat with the remaining nectarines.

Arrange the slices in a single layer in the prepared pan. Sprinkle the brown sugar evenly over the top and set aside.

In a bowl, beat the eggs with the granulated sugar until thick and pale. Using a rubber spatula, fold in the flour, then the melted butter and vanilla. Pour the batter over the fruit in the pan, spreading it evenly.

Bake until well browned and the juices are bubbling, 45–50 minutes. Remove from the oven and let cool on a rack for 5 minutes. Run a knife around the inside edge of the pan to loosen the cake sides. Invert a serving plate over the pan, then carefully flip the pan and plate together. Lift off the pan. Serve warm or at room temperature. ✷

Whole-Lemon Tart

SERVES 6–8

With a mandoline, you can easily cut the paper-thin slices you need to make this elegantly simple tart. The lemons are combined with sugar and macerated overnight, making them tender, sweet, and entirely edible. For the best flavor, serve this tart on the day that it is made.

2 thin-skinned lemons, well rinsed and dried

1 1/4 cups (10 oz/315 g) sugar

FOR THE PASTRY

1 cup (5 oz/155 g) all-purpose (plain) flour

1/2 cup (4 oz/125 g) cold unsalted butter, cut into small pieces

1 tablespoon sugar

1/8 teaspoon salt

2 eggs

Trim the ends from the lemons and cut the lemons in half crosswise. Set the straight edge of the slicing blade for the thinnest possible slices and slice the lemons, removing the seeds as you go. In a bowl, combine the lemons and the sugar. Cover and let stand overnight at room temperature.

Preheat an oven to 350°F (180°C).

To make the pastry, in a food processor, combine the flour, butter, sugar, and salt. Pulse 5 or 6 times, then process until the dough forms a ball. Transfer the dough to a work surface. Pinch off walnut-sized pieces of dough and press them evenly into the bottom and sides of a 9-inch (23-cm) tart pan with a removable bottom. Bake the pastry shell until pale golden, about 10 minutes. Transfer to a rack and let cool completely.

Raise the oven temperature to 375°F (190°C).

In a bowl, beat the eggs until blended but not foamy. Stir into
the lemon-sugar mixture and pour into the cooled pastry shell.
Straighten out any curly lemon slices, and shift the slices as
needed to make an even yet random layer.

Bake until the filling is set and the tart is golden brown on top,
25–30 minutes. Transfer to a rack and let cool, then remove the
pan sides and let cool completely. Slide onto a serving plate and
cut into wedges to serve. ✳

Apple Galette

SERVES 6–8

*Some restaurant chefs use an electric meat slicer to cut
the wafer-thin apple slices for this delectable tart. Home cooks
can use a mandoline to make slices that are equally thin.
Leave the peel on the apples; it adds color and flavor to this
astonishingly easy dessert.*

1 sheet (8 oz/250 g) puff pastry, thawed if frozen

3 tablespoons sugar

2 or 3 tart red apples such as Jonagold, Winesap,
or Gravenstein, cut into quarters and cored

Preheat an oven to 450°F (230°C).

On a lightly floured work surface, roll out the pastry into a
12-inch (30-cm) square and place on a large baking sheet. Turn
up the edges of the pastry to form a $^1/_2$-inch (12-mm) rim, pinch-
ing the corners together. Sprinkle 1 tablespoon of the sugar
evenly over the pastry.

87

Set the straight edge of the slicing blade for the thinnest possible slices and slice the apples. Discard any imperfect pieces.
Lay the slices, closely overlapping, on the pastry sheet. Sprinkle
the apple slices with the remaining 2 tablespoons sugar.

Place the tart in the oven and immediately reduce the temperature to 400°F (200°C). Bake until well browned, about 20 minutes. Serve hot or at room temperature. ✳

Winter Fruit and Custard Pie

MAKES ONE 9-INCH (23-CM) PIE

*Fine strips of pears, quickly cut with the julienne blade,
combine with lemon-scented custard, ginger, cranberries,
and chunks of prune in a lattice-top pie glamorous
enough for any holiday gathering.*

FOR THE PASTRY

2 oz (60 g) blanched almonds

1 1/2 cups (7 1/2 oz/235 g) all-purpose (plain) flour

1/4 teaspoon salt

1/2 cup (4 oz/125 g) cold unsalted butter, cut into small pieces

3 tablespoons ice water, or as needed

2 eggs

1/2 cup (4 oz/125 g) sugar

1/3 cup (3 fl oz/80 ml) heavy (double) cream

1/4 cup (1 oz/30 g) all-purpose (plain) flour

zest of 1 lemon

2 firm, ripe pears such as Anjou or Comice, about 1 lb
(500 g) total weight, peeled, halved lengthwise, and cored

1 piece fresh ginger, 1 inch (2.5 cm) long, peeled

1/2 cup (3 oz/90 g) soft pitted prunes, cut into quarters

1/2 cup (2 oz/60 g) fresh cranberries
or 1/4 cup (1 oz/30 g) dried cranberries

To make the pastry, in a food processor, grind the almonds to
a fine meal. Add the flour and salt and process to mix. Add the
butter and pulse until pea-sized pieces form. With the motor
running, add the ice water and process just until the dough
begins to hold together, adding more water by teaspoonfuls, if
needed. Remove the dough from the work bowl and divide into
2 portions, one twice as large as the other. Flatten each portion
into a disk.

On a floured work surface, roll out the larger dough portion into an 11-inch (28-cm) round. Fit into a 9-inch (23-cm) pie pan, allowing the dough to extend ½ inch (12 mm) over the edge. Roll out the remaining dough into a 9-inch (23-cm) round and cut into strips ½ inch (12 mm) wide for the lattice top. Place them on a flat pan, cover with plastic wrap, and refrigerate, along with the pastry-lined pie pan, while you prepare the filling.

Preheat an oven to 400°F (200°C).

In a bowl, whisk together the eggs, sugar, cream, flour, and lemon zest until smooth.

Insert the ⅛-inch (3-mm) julienne blade next to the straight edge of the slicing blade and set the guiding plate to a thickness of ⅛ inch (3 mm). Starting with the wide end, cut the pears crosswise into julienne strips. As they are cut, transfer the pear strips to the egg mixture. If the ginger is very tender, slice it lengthwise into julienne. If the ginger is fibrous, remove the julienne blade, put the serrated edge of the slicing blade in place, and shred the ginger, rotating it a quarter turn at a time. Discard any woody part at the center. Add to the egg mixture along with the prunes and cranberries. Mix well.

Pour the filling into the pastry-lined pie pan. Moisten the rim of the crust with cold water. Arrange the pastry strips across the top in a lattice pattern. Press the ends of the strips firmly against the rim of the crust. Fold the overhanging pastry over the top and press together, using your thumb and forefinger to make a fluted edge.

Bake until the filling is set and the crust is brown, about 45 minutes. Let cool completely on a rack.

Cut into wedges and serve at room temperature. ✳

Ambrosia

SERVES 6

*Many markets sell coconuts and pineapples already cut
in half, which means less work and less waste.*

$1/2$ coconut, about $1/2$ lb (250 g)

2 navel oranges, about 1 $1/2$ lb (750 g) total weight

$1/2$ ripe pineapple, about 1 $1/2$ lb (750 g)

4–6 tablespoons (2–3 oz/60–90 g) sugar

1 tablespoon Grand Marnier or other orange-flavored liqueur

Break the coconut into 1-by-2-inch (2.5-by-5-cm) pieces. Set
the serrated edge of the slicing blade for the thinnest possible
slices. Place the coconut pieces, meat sides down, on the guiding plate and finely shred the coconut meat; you will need about
$3/4$ cup (2 oz/60 g). Pass 1 of the oranges across the shredder
plate to yield 1 teaspoon shredded zest.

Trim off both ends of the pineapple half and discard. Cut the
pineapple half in half lengthwise and remove the core. Halve
each piece lengthwise again. Using a sharp knife, remove the
rind. Cut the trimmed sections crosswise into 3-inch (7.5-cm)
lengths. Set the straight edge of the slicing blade for $1/8$ inch
(3 mm). Slice the pineapple pieces crosswise.

Using a small, sharp knife, cut a slice off the top and bottom of
each orange. Place the oranges upright on a cutting board. Slice
off the peel in thick strips, cutting around the contour of the
oranges to expose the flesh. Set the straight edge of the slicing
blade for $1/4$ inch (6 mm) and slice the oranges crosswise.

In a serving bowl, make a layer of one-third of the pineapple.
Sprinkle it with about 1 tablespoon of the sugar (the amount
depends upon the sweetness of the pineapple) and one-sixth
of the coconut and the orange zest. Top with a layer of orange
slices, 1 tablespoon sugar, and one-sixth of the coconut. Repeat
the layers two more times, ending with coconut. Drizzle the
liqueur over the top.

Cover with plastic wrap and refrigerate overnight or for up to
3 days before serving. ✳

Ginger Shortcakes with Melon and Tropical Fruits

SERVES 6

Look for carambola, sometimes called starfruit, from August through mid-February. Thick, fleshy ribs indicate the sweeter varieties, and a fruity, floral aroma means that the fruit is ripe and ready to eat.

I carambola

1 ½ cups (12 oz/375 g) sugar

1 ¼ cups (10 fl oz/310 ml) water

I honeydew melon, about I lb (500 g)

I cantaloupe, about I lb (500 g)

2 tablespoons lime juice

I tablespoon finely shredded orange zest

½ cup (4 fl oz/125 ml) orange juice

FOR THE SHORTCAKES

I cup (5 oz/155 g) all-purpose (plain) flour

1 ½ teaspoons baking powder

¼ teaspoon salt

¼ cup (2 oz/60 g) unsalted butter

½ cup (4 fl oz/125 ml) heavy (double) cream

3 tablespoons preserved ginger in syrup, drained and finely chopped

I kiwifruit

Cut the carambola in half crosswise. Set the straight edge of the slicing blade for ⅛ inch (3 mm). Slice the carambola. Discard any seeds.

In a nonaluminum saucepan over medium heat, combine 1 cup (8 oz/250 g) of the sugar and the water. Bring to a boil, stirring to dissolve the sugar. Reduce the heat and simmer until clear, about 5 minutes. Add the carambola slices and simmer until translucent, about 5 minutes. Transfer to a bowl.

Cut the melons in half and discard the seeds. Cut each half into wedges 1 inch (2.5 cm) wide, then peel the wedges. Set the straight edge of the slicing blade for $1/4$ inch (6 mm) and slice the melon wedges crosswise. Add the melon and lime juice to the bowl holding the carambola. Let cool completely, cover, and refrigerate for several hours.

In the same saucepan over medium-high heat, combine the orange zest, orange juice, and the remaining $1/2$ cup (4 oz/125 g) sugar. Bring to a boil, reduce the heat to low, and simmer until slightly thickened, about 5 minutes. Remove from the heat and set aside.

Preheat an oven to 450°F (230°C).

To make the shortcakes, in a medium bowl, stir together the flour, baking powder, and salt. Add the butter and, using a pastry blender, cut it in until the mixture resembles coarse meal. Add the cream and chopped ginger, stirring lightly with a fork until a soft dough forms. Turn out the dough onto a floured work surface and knead lightly to form a smooth ball. Roll or pat out the dough into a 4-by-9-inch (10-by-23-cm) rectangle about $1/2$ inch (12 mm) thick. Cut crosswise into 3 equal pieces, then cut each piece from corner to corner to make 6 triangles. Place 1 inch (2.5 cm) apart on an ungreased baking sheet.

Bake until golden brown, 10–12 minutes. Remove the baking sheet from the oven and place on a rack to cool slightly.

To serve, peel the kiwifruit. Set the straight edge of the slicing blade for $1/4$ inch (6 mm) and slice the kiwifruit. Divide the slices among individual plates. Using a slotted spoon, transfer the melon and carambola slices to the plates. Drizzle the orange sauce over each portion, dividing evenly. Place a warm shortcake on the other half of each plate and serve. ✳

INDEX

ACKNOWLEDGMENTS

The author would like to thank chef instructor Catherine Brandel of the Culinary Institute of America at Greystone, who came to love the mandoline at a time when a cast on her arm made knife work impossible. Her enthusiasm is at the heart of this project.